# Pocket Edition 100 FACTS

# SPACE

# Pocket Edition 100 FACTS
# SPACE

Sue Becklake

Consultant: Peter Bond

Miles Kelly

First published in 2002 by Miles Kelly Publishing Ltd
Harding's Barn, Bardfield End Green, Thaxted, Essex, CM6 3PX, UK

This edition updated 2013, published 2018, printed 2019

2 4 6 8 10 9 7 5 3


PUBLISHING DIRECTOR Belinda Gallagher
CREATIVE DIRECTOR Jo Cowan
EDITORIAL DIRECTOR Rosie Neave
DESIGNER Rob Hale
COVER DESIGNER Simon Lee
PRODUCTION Elizabeth Collins, Jennifer Brunwin-Jones
REPROGRAPHICS Stephan Davis, Callum Ratcliffe-Bingham
ASSETS Lorraine King

ISBN 978-1-78617-624-0

Printed in China

British Library Cataloguing-in-Publication Data
A catalogue record for this book is available from the British Library

**ACKNOWLEDGEMENTS**
The publishers would like to thank the following sources for the use of their photographs:
Key: t = top, b = bottom, c = centre, l = left, r = right, m = main, bg = background

**Cover** (front) Victor Habbick Visions/Science Photo Library,
(back) (t) xello/Shutterstock, (cbg) Olegusk/Shutterstock, (cl) Rafael Pacheco/Shutterstock
**Istock** 13(b) 101cats
**Digital Vision** 34(bl); 46(tr)
**NASA Images** 8(tl), (bl), (bc); 9(cl) The Exploratorium; 13(tr), (br) JPL-Caltech; 14(tr) JPL/USGS, 14(b) JPL; 15(tr), (bl);
16(br) Johns Hopkins University Applied Physics Laboratory/Carnegie Institution of Washington; 18(c) JPL/University of Arizona,
(bl), (br); 19(tr) JPL/Space Science Institute, (bl) E. Karkoschka (University of Arizona); 20(tl) ESA, and L. Lamy (Observatory of Paris,
CNRS, CNES), 21(cl); 25(tr) ESA/STScI; 26(tr), (bl) ESA, K. Noll (STScI), (br) H. Richer (University of British Columbia); 27 (tr) JPL-Caltech/
STScI/CXC/SAO, (br) NASA/CXC; 29(tr), (tl) CXC/KIPAC/S.Allen et al; Radio: NRAO/VLA/G.Taylor; Infrared: NASA/ESA/McMaster
Univ./W.Harris; (cl) ESA, and the Hubble Heritage (STScI/AURA)-ESA/Hubble Collaboration, (bl) ESA, A. Nota (ESA/STScI) et al, (br) ESA,
M. Livio (STScI) and the Hubble Heritage Team (STScI/AURA); 30(bl) ESA, M. Postman (STScI), and the CLASH Team, (cr); 33(t); 35(l),
(m) Dick Clark; 36(tr); 37(b); 39(tr); 41(tr); 44(t); 45(m); 46(l)
**PhotoDisc** 4(tc); 6–7; 8(br); 16(l) **Science Photo Library** 17(m) Mark Garlick, 24–25(m) Mark Garlick
**Shutterstock** 9(bl) Dimec; 12(bl) tororo reaction; 22 MarcelClemens; 23(b) Action Sports Photography; 28(m) John A Davis;
32(tr/cl) Eky Studio, (br) Karin Wassmer; 33(m) Manamana; 46(cr) Elisei Shafer, (cr) Thomas Barrat, (br) javarman

All artworks are from the Miles Kelly Artwork Bank

All other photographs are from:

digitalSTOCK, digitalvision, Dreamstime.com, Fotolia.com, iStockphoto.com,
John Foxx, PhotoAlto, PhotoDisc, PhotoEssentials, PhotoPro, Stockbyte

Every effort has been made to acknowledge the source and copyright holder of each picture.
Miles Kelly Publishing apologizes for any unintentional errors or omissions.

Made with paper from a sustainable forest

www.mileskelly.net

The publishers would like to thank the Society for Popular Astronomy for their help in compiling this book.

# Contents

Surrounded by space  6

Our life-giving star  8

A family of planets  10

Planet of life  12

The Earth's neighbours  14

The smallest of all  16

The biggest of all  18

So far away  20

Comets, asteroids and meteors  22

A star is born  24

Death of a star  26

Billions of galaxies  28

What is the Universe?  30

Looking into space  32

Three, two, one… lift-off!  34

Living in space  36

Home from home  38

Robot explorers  40

Watching the Earth  42

Voyage to the Moon  44

Are we alone?  46

Index  48

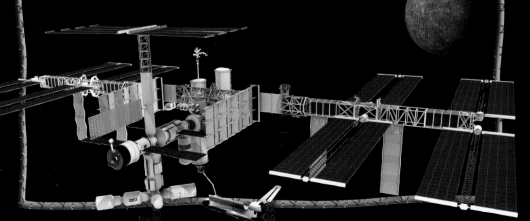

**1** **Space is all around Earth, high above the air.** Here on Earth we are surrounded by air. If you go upwards – for example, by climbing a high mountain or flying in a plane – the air grows thinner until there is none at all. Space officially begins 100 kilometres up from sea level. It is mostly empty, but there are many exciting things such as planets, stars and galaxies. People who travel in space are called astronauts.

▶ In space, astronauts wear spacesuits to go outside a space station or a spacecraft as it circles Earth. Much farther away are planets, stars and galaxies.

# Our life-giving star

**2** The Sun is our nearest star. Most stars are so far away they look like points of light in the sky, but the Sun looks different because it is much closer to us. The Sun is not solid, like Earth. It is a huge ball of super-hot gases, so hot that they glow like the flames of a bonfire.

◀ The Sun's hot, glowing gas is always on the move, bubbling up to the surface and sinking back down again.

**3** Nothing could live on Earth without the Sun. Deep in its centre the Sun is constantly making energy that keeps its gases hot and glowing. This energy works its way to the surface where it escapes as heat and light. Without it, Earth would be cold and dark with no life at all.

## PROMINENCE

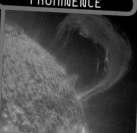

Solar prominences can reach temperatures of 10,000°C.

## SOLAR FLARE

Solar flares erupt in a few minutes, then take more than half an hour to die away again.

## SUNSPOT

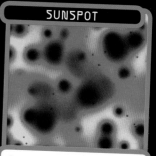

Groups of sunspots seem to move across the Sun over two weeks, as the Sun rotates.

**4** The Sun is often spotty. Sunspots appear on the surface, some wider than Earth. They look dark because they are cooler than the rest of the Sun. Solar flares – explosions of energy – can suddenly shoot out from the Sun. The Sun also throws huge loops of gas called prominences out into space.

▶ When the Moon casts a shadow on Earth, there is a solar eclipse.

**5** When the Moon hides the Sun there is a solar eclipse. Every so often, the Sun, Moon and Earth line up in space so that the Moon comes directly between the Earth and the Sun. This stops the sunlight from reaching a small area on Earth. This area grows dark and cold, as if night has come early.

▲ A photo of a solar eclipse on I August 2008 shows the Moon totally blocking the Sun, and reveals the Sun's halo-like corona – part of its atmosphere not normally seen because the Sun's surface is too bright.

### I DON'T BELIEVE IT!
The surface of the Sun is nearly 60 times hotter than boiling water. It is so hot it would melt a spacecraft flying near it.

# A family of planets

**6** The Sun is surrounded by a family of circling planets called the Solar System. This family is held together by an invisible force called gravity, which pulls things towards each other. It is the same force that pulls us down to the ground and stops us from floating away. The Sun's gravity pulls on the planets and keeps them circling around it.

**I DON'T BELIEVE IT!**
If the Sun was the size of a large beach ball, Earth would be as small as a pea, and the Moon would look like a pinhead.

JUPITER

MARS

VENUS

EARTH

MERCURY

SUN

**7** Earth is one of eight planets in the Sun's family. They all circle the Sun at different distances from it. The four planets nearest to the Sun are all balls of rock. The other four planets are much bigger and are made of gas and liquid.

▼ The eight planets are all different. Mercury, nearest the Sun, is small and hot. Then Venus, Earth and Mars are rocky and cooler. Beyond them Jupiter, Saturn, Uranus and Neptune are large and cold.

NEPTUNE

URANUS

SATURN

**8** Moons circle the planets, travelling with them round the Sun. Earth has one moon. It circles Earth while Earth circles round the Sun. Mars has two tiny moons, but Mercury and Venus have none at all. There are large families of moons, like miniature solar systems, around all the large gas planets.

**9** There are millions of smaller members in the Sun's family. Some are tiny specks of dust speeding through space between the planets. Larger chunks of rock, many as large as mountains, are called asteroids. Comets come from the edge of the Solar System, skimming past the Sun before they disappear again.

# Planet of life

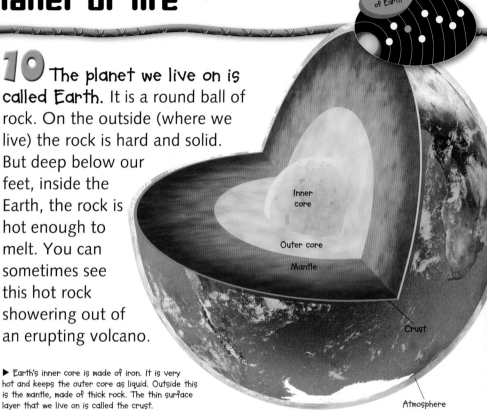

**10** **The planet we live on is called Earth.** It is a round ball of rock. On the outside (where we live) the rock is hard and solid. But deep below our feet, inside the Earth, the rock is hot enough to melt. You can sometimes see this hot rock showering out of an erupting volcano.

Inner core

Outer core

Mantle

Crust

Atmosphere

▶ Earth's inner core is made of iron. It is very hot and keeps the outer core as liquid. Outside this is the mantle, made of thick rock. The thin surface layer that we live on is called the crust.

▼ No other planet in the Solar System has liquid water on its surface, so Earth is the only known planet suitable for life.

**11** **Earth is the only planet with life.** From space, Earth is a blue-and-white planet, with huge oceans and wet masses of cloud. Animals – including people – and plants can live on Earth because of all this water.

**12** Sunshine gives us daylight when it is night on the other side of the Earth. When it is daytime, your part of the Earth faces towards the Sun and it is light. At night, your part faces away from the Sun and it is dark. Day follows night because the Earth is always turning.

As Earth rotates, the day and night halves shift gradually around the world. Earth turns eastwards, so the Sun rises in the east as each part of the world spins to face it.

**13** Craters on the Moon are scars from space rocks crashing into the surface. When a rock smashes into the Moon at high speed, it leaves a saucer-shaped dent, pushing some of the rock outwards into a ring of mountains.

**14** Look for the Moon on clear nights and watch how it seems to change shape. Over a month it changes from a thin crescent to a round shape. This is because sunlight is reflected by the Moon. We see the full Moon when the sunlit side faces Earth and a thin, crescent shape when most of the sunlit side is facing away from us.

Crescent moon

Half moon

Full moon

Half moon

Crescent moon

▲ During the first half of each monthly cycle, the Moon waxes (appears to grow). During the second half, it wanes (dwindles) back to a crescent-shape.

▲ Dark patches are called seas although there is no water on the Moon.

# The Earth's neighbours

**15** Venus and Mars are the nearest planets to Earth. Venus is closer to the Sun than Earth while Mars is farther away. Each takes a different amount of time to circle the Sun and we call this its year. A year on Venus is 225 days, on Earth 365 days and on Mars 687 days.

**16** Venus is the hottest planet, even though Mercury is closer to the Sun. Heat builds up on Venus because it is completely covered by clouds that trap the heat, like the glass in a greenhouse.

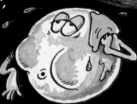

▲ Dense clouds surround Venus, making it difficult to observe, so the *Magellan* spacecraft spent four years mapping the surface with radar (bouncing radio waves) to produce images like this.

▲ Under its clouds, Venus has hundreds of volcanoes, large and small, all over its surface. We do not know if any of them are still erupting.

**17** The clouds around Venus are poisonous — they contain drops of acid that would burn your skin. They are not like clouds on Earth, which are made of droplets of water. They are thick, and do not let much sunshine reach the surface of Venus.

Solar panel

Camera

Radio aerial

**18** Winds on Mars whip up huge dust storms that can cover the whole planet. Mars is very dry, like a desert, and covered in red dust. When a space probe called *Mariner 9* arrived there in 1971, the whole planet was hidden by dust clouds.

▲ *Mariner 9* was the first space probe to circle another planet. Since that time more than 30 other crafts have travelled onto Mars and several have soft-landed including 4 rovers.

**19** Mars has the largest volcano in the Solar System. It is called Olympus Mons and is three times as high as Mount Everest, the tallest mountain on Earth. Olympus Mons is an old volcano and it has not erupted for millions of years.

## LIFE ON MARS
Mars is the best known planet besides Earth. It is dry, rocky and covered in dust. Look in books and on the Internet to find out more about Mars. What do you think it would be like to live there?

**20** There are plans to send astronauts to Mars but the journey would take six months or more. The astronauts would have to take with them everything they need for the journey there and back and for their stay on Mars.

◄ The Hubble Space Telescope has captured a giant dust storm in this picture of Mars. The bright orange patch in the middle shows where the dry red dust is blown up by strong winds.

# The smallest of all

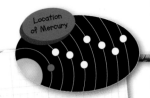
**21** Mercury looks like our Moon. It is a round, cratered ball of rock. Although a little larger than the Moon, like the Moon it has no air.

## MAKE CRATERS

**You will need:**
flour   baking tray
a marble or a stone

1. Spread some flour about 2 centimetres deep on a baking tray and smooth over the surface.
2. Drop a marble or a small round stone onto the flour.
3. Can you see the saucer-shaped crater the marble makes?

◀ Mercury has high cliffs and long ridges as well as craters. Astronomers think it cooled and shrank in the past, making its surface wrinkled.

### CRATERS

Mercury's many craters show how often it was hit by space rocks. One was so large that it shattered rocks on the other side of the planet.

**22** The sunny side of Mercury is boiling hot but the night side is freezing cold. Being the nearest planet to the Sun, the sunny side can get twice as hot as an oven. But Mercury spins round slowly so the night side has time to cool down, and there is no air to trap the heat. The night side becomes more than twice as cold as Antarctica – the coldest place on Earth.

**23** Tiny, rocky Pluto was discovered in 1930. At first it was called a planet, but in 2006, it was re-classified as a dwarf planet. It is less than half the width of Mercury. In fact, Pluto is smaller than our Moon.

**25** Aside from Pluto, four other dwarf planets have been named. They are called Ceres, Eris, Makemake and Haumea (in order from the closest to the Sun to the farthest away). Eris is larger than Pluto.

CERES

PLUTO

ERIS

▲ Ceres orbits between Mars and Jupiter. Pluto orbits further away from the Sun than Neptune, and Eris is further out still.

**24** If you stood on the surface of Pluto, the Sun would not look much brighter than any other stars. Pluto is so far from the Sun that it receives little heat and is completely covered in ice.

**26** New Horizons is the first space probe to visit Pluto. It blasted off in 2006 and reached the dwarf planet in July. If all goes well it will then carry on to the outer region of the Solar System, called the Kuiper Belt.

# The biggest of all

**27** **Jupiter is more massive than the other seven planets in the Solar System put together.** It is 11 times as wide as Earth, although it is still much smaller than the Sun. Saturn, the next largest planet, is more than nine times as wide as the Earth.

**28** **Jupiter has more than 60 moons.** Its moon Io has many active volcanoes that throw out huge plumes of material, making red blotches and dark marks on its orange-yellow surface.

**29** **The Great Red Spot on Jupiter is a 300-year-old storm.** It was first noticed about 300 years ago and is at least twice as wide as the Earth. It rises above the rest of the clouds and swirls around like storm clouds on Earth.

◀ Jupiter's fast winds blow clouds into coloured bands around the planet.

▼ There are many storms on Jupiter but none are as large or long-lasting as the Great Red Spot.

Io

Europa

Ganymede

Callisto

These four large moons were discovered by Galileo Galilei in 1610, which is why they are known as the Galilean moons.

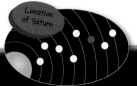

Location of Saturn

▶ Although Saturn's rings are very wide, they stretch out in a very thin layer around the planet.

**30** The shining rings around Saturn are made of millions of chunks of ice. These circle the planet like tiny moons and shine by reflecting sunlight from their surfaces. Some are as small as ice cubes while others are as large as a car.

**31** Jupiter and Saturn are gas giants. They have no solid surface for a spacecraft to land on. All that you can see are the tops of their clouds. Beneath the clouds, the planets are made mostly of gas (like air) and liquid (water is a liquid).

▼ Taken with the Hubble Space Telescope, this image shows a detailed view of Saturn's southern hemisphere and its rings.

**I DON'T BELIEVE IT!**
For its size, Saturn is lighter than any other planet. If there was a large enough sea, it would float like a cork.

**32** Jupiter and Saturn spin round so fast that they bulge out in the middle. This can happen because they are not made of solid rock. As they spin, their clouds are stretched out into light and dark bands around them.

# So far away

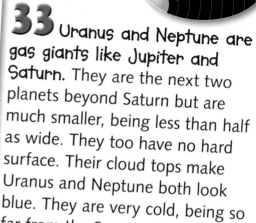

Location of Uranus

▲ This photo shows an aurora display (the glowing blue dot) on Uranus. Aurorae are made by tiny particles given off by the Sun, known as the solar wind. These get trapped by a planet's magnetism and start to glow.

**33** Uranus and Neptune are gas giants like Jupiter and Saturn. They are the next two planets beyond Saturn but are much smaller, being less than half as wide. They too have no hard surface. Their cloud tops make Uranus and Neptune both look blue. They are very cold, being so far from the Sun.

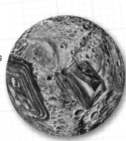

▶ Uranus's moon Miranda looks as though it has been split apart and put back together again.

**34** Uranus seems to 'roll' around the Sun. Most of the other planets spin upright like tops, but Uranus spins on its side. It may have been knocked over when something crashed into it millions of years ago.

▼ Uranus's five largest moons are big enough to be classified as dwarf planets, but they are not in direct orbit of the Sun.

| | NAME | DIAMETER | YEAR OF DISCOVERY |
|---|---|---|---|
| 1 | Titania | 1578 km | 1787 |
| 2 | Oberon | 1523 km | 1787 |
| 3 | Umbriel | 1169 km | 1851 |
| 4 | Ariel | 1158 km | 1851 |
| 5 | Miranda | 472 km | 1948 |

**35** Uranus has more than 25 moons, and there are probably more to be discovered. Most are very small, but Titania, the largest, is 1578 kilometres across, which makes it the eighth largest moon in the Solar System.

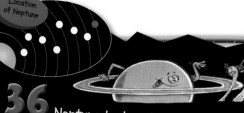

# 36
**Neptune had a storm that disappeared.** When the *Voyager 2* space probe flew past Neptune in 1989 it spotted a huge storm, like a dark version of the Great Red Spot on Jupiter. But when the Hubble Space Telescope looked at Neptune in 1994, the storm had gone.

▲ *Voyager 2* is the only probe to visit Neptune and send back close up pictures of the planet.

# 37
**Neptune has bright blue clouds that make the whole planet look blue.** Above them are smaller white streaks – icy clouds that race around the planet. One of these clouds, seen by the *Voyager 2* space probe, was named 'Scooter' because it scooted around the planet so fast.

# 38
**Neptune is sometimes farther from the Sun than Pluto.** Planets and dwarf planets go around the Sun on orbits (paths) that look like circles, but Pluto's path is more squashed. This sometimes brings it closer to the Sun than Neptune.

Orbit of Pluto

Sun

Neptune

Pluto

Orbit of Neptune

▲ Neptune is so far from the Sun that its orbit lasts 164.79 Earth years. It has only completed one orbit since it was discovered in 1846.

**39** There are probably billions of tiny comets at the edge of the Solar System. They circle the Sun far beyond Neptune. Sometimes one is disturbed and moves inwards towards the Sun, looping around it before going back to where it came from. Some comets come back to the Sun regularly – Halley's comet returns every 76 years.

The solid part of a comet is hidden inside a huge, glowing cloud that stretches into a long tail.

**40** A comet is often called a dirty snowball because it is made of dust and ice mixed together. Heat from the Sun melts some of the ice. This makes dust and gas stream away from the comet, forming a huge tail that glows in the sunlight.

**41** Comet tails always point away from the Sun. Although it looks bright, a comet's tail is extremely thin so it is blown outwards, away from the Sun. When the comet moves away from the Sun, its tail goes in front of it.

**42** **Asteroids are chunks of rock that failed to stick together to make a planet.** Most of them circle the Sun between Mars and Jupiter where there would be room for another planet. There are millions of asteroids, some the size of a car, and others as big as mountains.

**ASTEROIDS**

**43** **Meteors are sometimes called shooting stars.** They are not really stars, just streaks of light that flash across the night sky. Meteors are made when pebbles racing through space at high speed hit the top of the air above the Earth. The pebble gets so hot it burns up. We see it as a glowing streak for a few seconds.

Asteroids travel in a ring around the Sun. This ring is called the asteroid belt and can be found between Mars and Jupiter.

▼ This crater in Arizona is one of the few large meteorite craters visible on Earth. The Moon is covered in them.

# QUIZ

1. Which way does a comet tail always point?

2. What is another name for a meteor?

3. Where is the asteroid belt?

Answers:
1. Away from the Sun
2. Shooting star
3. Between Mars and Jupiter

# A star is born

**44** Stars are born in clouds of dust and gas called nebulae. Astronomers can see these clouds as shining patches in the night sky, or dark patches against the distant stars. These clouds shrink as gravity pulls the dust and gas together. At the centre, the gas gets hotter and hotter until a new star is born.

**45** Stars begin their lives when they start making energy. When the dust and gas pulls tightly together it gets very hot. Finally it gets so hot in the middle that it can start making energy. The energy makes the star shine, giving out heat and light like the Sun.

## QUIZ

1. What is a nebula?
2. How long has the Sun been shining?
3. What colour are large hot stars?
4. What is a group of new young stars called?

Answers:
1. A cloud of dust and gas in space 2. About 4.6 billion years 3. Bluish-white 4. Star cluster

## KEY

**1** Clumps of gas in a nebula start to shrink into the tight round balls that will become stars. The gas spirals round as it is pulled inwards.

**2** Deep in its centre, the new star starts making energy, but it is still hidden by the cloud of dust and gas.

**3** The dust and gas are blown away and we can see the star shining. Any left over gas and dust may form planets around the new star.

**46** Young stars often stay together in clusters. When they start to shine they light up the nebula, making it glow with bright colours. Then the starlight blows away the remains of the cloud and we can see a group of new stars, called a star cluster.

**47** Large stars are very hot and white, smaller stars are cooler and redder. A large star can make energy faster and get much hotter than a smaller star. This gives them a very bright, bluish-white colour. Smaller stars are cooler. This makes them look red and shine less brightly. Ordinary in-between stars – like our Sun – look yellow.

STAR CLUSTER

This cluster of young stars, with many stars of different colours and sizes, will gradually drift apart, breaking up the cluster.

**48** Smaller stars live much longer than huge stars. Stars use up their gas to make energy, and the largest stars use up their gas much faster than smaller stars. The Sun is about halfway through its life. It has been shining for about 4.6 billion years and will go on shining for another 5 billion years.

②

③

# Death of a star

**49** Stars begin to die when they run out of gas to make energy. The middle of the star begins to shrink but the outer parts expand, making the star much larger.

At the end of their lives stars swell up into red giant stars, as shown in this far infrared image, or even larger red supergiants.

**50** Red giant stars are dying stars that have swollen to hundreds of times their normal size. Their expanding outer layers get cooler, making them look red. When the Sun is a red giant it will be large enough to swallow up the nearest planets, Mercury and Venus, and perhaps Earth.

**51** Eventually, a red giant's outer layers drift away, making a halo of gas around the star. The starlight makes this gas glow and we call it a planetary nebula. All that is left is a small, hot star called a white dwarf, which cannot make energy and gradually cools and dies.

PLANETARY NEBULA

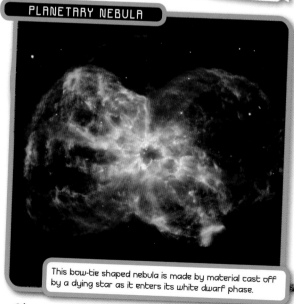

This bow-tie shaped nebula is made by material cast off by a dying star as it enters its white dwarf phase.

WHITE DWARF STARS

These ancient white dwarf stars are in our Milky Way Galaxy, and are between 12 and 13 billion years old.

**52** Very heavy stars end their lives in a huge explosion called a supernova. This explosion blows away all the outer parts of the star. All that is left is a tiny hot star in the middle of a shell of hot glowing gas.

▶ Cassiopeia A is one of the best-studied supernova remnants. This image was made using data from three different types of telescopes.

## I DON'T BELIEVE IT!

One of the main signs of a black hole is radiation from very hot gases near one just before they are sucked in.

**53** After a supernova explosion the largest stars may end up as black holes. The remains of the star fall in on itself. As it shrinks, its gravity gets stronger. Eventually the pull of its gravity can get so strong that nothing near it can escape. This is called a black hole.

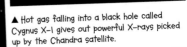

▲ Hot gas falling into a black hole called Cygnus X-1 gives out powerful X-rays picked up by the Chandra satellite.

**54** The Sun is part of a huge family of stars called the Milky Way Galaxy. There are billions of other stars in our galaxy, as many as the grains of sand on a beach. We call it the Milky Way because it looks like a very faint band of light in the night sky, as though someone has spilt some milk across space.

▶ With binoculars you can see that the faint glow of the Milky Way comes from millions of stars in our galaxy.

**55** Curling arms give some galaxies their spiral shape. The Milky Way has arms made of bright stars and glowing clouds of gas that curl round into a spiral shape. Some galaxies, called elliptical galaxies, have a round shape like a squashed ball. Other galaxies have no particular shape.

**I DON'T BELIEVE IT!**
If you could fit the Milky Way onto these two pages, the Sun would be so tiny, you could not see it.

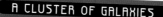

**56** There are billions of galaxies outside the Milky Way. Some are larger than the Milky Way and many are smaller, but they all have more stars than you can count. The galaxies tend to stay together in groups called clusters.

Astronomers have nicknamed this interesting cluster of galaxies the 'Bullet Cluster'. It is made up of two colliding groups of galaxies.

### ELLIPTICAL

### SPIRAL

### IRREGULAR

▲ Galaxies can be categorized by their shape. The Milky Way is a spiral galaxy.

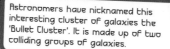

**57** There is no bump when galaxies collide. A galaxy is mostly empty space between the stars. But when galaxies get very close they can pull each other out of shape. Sometimes they look as if they have grown a huge tail stretching out into space, or their shape may change into a ring of glowing stars.

▲ These two galaxies are so close that each has pulled a long tail of bright stars from the other.

# What is the Universe?

**58** **The Universe is the name we give to everything we know about.** This means everything on Earth, from tiny bits of dust to the highest mountain, and everything that lives here. It also means everything in space – all the billions of stars in the billions of galaxies.

**59** **The Universe started with a massive explosion called the Big Bang.** Astronomers think that this happened about 13.7 billion years ago. The explosion sent everything racing outwards in all directions. To start with, everything was packed incredibly close together. Over time it has expanded (spread out) into the Universe we can see today, which is mostly empty space.

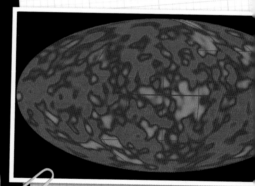

▲ A satellite has measured and mapped the oldest light in the Universe, known as the cosmic microwave background, providing a snapshot of the early Universe.

## DARK MATTER

Some of the distant galaxies in this cluster appear distorted, because light coming from them is being bent by invisible dark matter.

**60** **The Universe's matter includes planets, stars and gas, and its energy includes light and heat.** Scientists suspect that it also contains unknown dark matter and dark energy, which we are unable to detect. These may affect what finally happens to the Universe.

**61** The galaxies are still racing away from each other. When astronomers look at distant galaxies they can see that other galaxies are moving away from our galaxy, and the more distant galaxies are moving away faster. In fact all the galaxies are moving apart from each other. We say that the Universe is expanding.

**62** We do not know what will happen to the Universe billions of years in the future. It may keep on expanding. If this happens, old stars will gradually die and no new ones will be born. Everywhere will become dark and cold.

## DOTTY UNIVERSE

**You will need:**
balloon  pen
Blow up a balloon a little, holding the neck to stop air escaping. Mark dots on the balloon with a pen, then blow it up some more. Watch how the dots move apart from each other. This is like the galaxies moving apart as the Universe expands.

### KEY

❶ All the parts that make up the Universe were once packed tightly together. No one knows why the Universe started expanding with a Big Bang.

❷ As everything moved apart in all directions, stars and galaxies started to form.

❸ Today there are galaxies of different shapes and sizes, all moving apart. One day they may start moving towards each other.

❹ The Universe could stop expanding, or shrink and end with a Big Crunch.

# Looking into space

**63** People have imagined they can see the outlines of people and animals in the star patterns in the sky. These patterns are called constellations. Hundreds of years ago astronomers named the constellations to help them find their way around the skies.

◀ The constellation Scorpius (in the Southern Hemisphere) is easy to recognize because it looks like a scorpion with a curved tail.

▲ The constellation Orion (shown here in the Northern Hemisphere) is one of the most recognizable in the night sky.

**64** Astronomers use huge telescopes to see much more than we can see with just our eyes. Telescopes make things look bigger and nearer. They also show faint, glowing clouds of gas, and distant stars and galaxies.

▲ Mauna Kea observatory is situated on the summit of Mauna Kea on the US island of Hawaii. Telescopes are usually located high up, far from towns and cities so that they have a clear view of the skies.

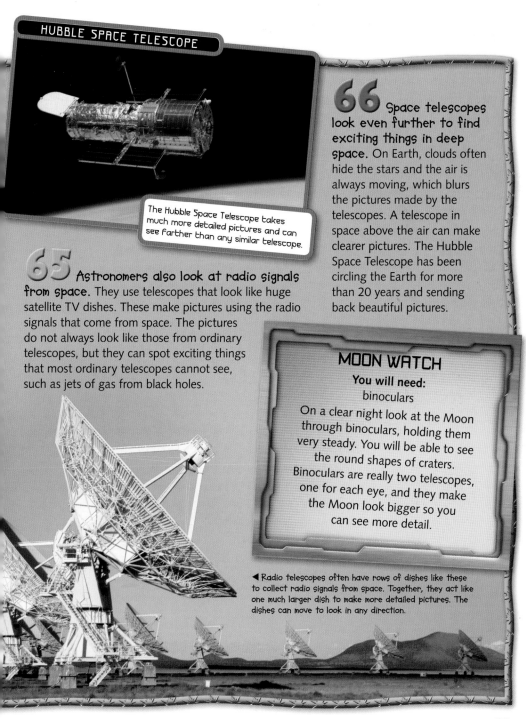

## HUBBLE SPACE TELESCOPE

The Hubble Space Telescope takes much more detailed pictures and can see farther than any similar telescope.

**66** Space telescopes look even further to find exciting things in deep space. On Earth, clouds often hide the stars and the air is always moving, which blurs the pictures made by the telescopes. A telescope in space above the air can make clearer pictures. The Hubble Space Telescope has been circling the Earth for more than 20 years and sending back beautiful pictures.

**65** Astronomers also look at radio signals from space. They use telescopes that look like huge satellite TV dishes. These make pictures using the radio signals that come from space. The pictures do not always look like those from ordinary telescopes, but they can spot exciting things that most ordinary telescopes cannot see, such as jets of gas from black holes.

### MOON WATCH
**You will need:**
binoculars
On a clear night look at the Moon through binoculars, holding them very steady. You will be able to see the round shapes of craters. Binoculars are really two telescopes, one for each eye, and they make the Moon look bigger so you can see more detail.

◀ Radio telescopes often have rows of dishes like these to collect radio signals from space. Together, they act like one much larger dish to make more detailed pictures. The dishes can move to look in any direction.

# Three, two, one... lift-off!

**67** **A rocket must travel nearly 40 times faster than a jumbo jet to blast into space.** Slower than that, and gravity will pull it back to Earth. Rockets are powered by burning fuel, which makes hot gases. These gases rush out of the engines, shooting the rocket upwards.

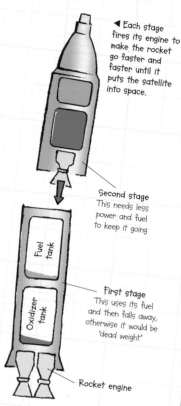

◄ Each stage fires its engine to make the rocket go faster and faster until it puts the satellite into space.

**Second stage**
This needs less power and fuel to keep it going

Fuel tank

**First stage**
This uses its fuel and then falls away, otherwise it would be 'dead weight'

Oxidizer tank

Rocket engine

This shuttle was blasted into space by three rocket engines and two huge booster rockets.

**68** **A single rocket is usually not powerful enough to launch a satellite or spacecraft.** So most have two or three stages, which are really separate rockets mounted on top of each other, each with its own engines. When the first stage has used up its fuel it drops away, and the second stage starts. Finally the third stage takes over to go into space.

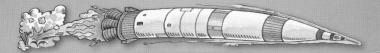

**69** Some launchers have boosters. These are extra rockets fixed to the main one. Most boosters burn solid fuel, like giant firework rockets. They fall away when the fuel has burnt up. Some drift down on parachutes into the sea, to be used again.

The shuttle puts down its wheels and lands on the runway. A parachute and speed brakes bring the shuttle to a standstill.

◄ On 8 July, 2011, space shuttle *Atlantis* took off from Florida, USA on the final mission of the 30-year space shuttle programme.

**70** The space shuttles were re-usable spaceplanes. The first was launched in 1981 and there were more than 130 missions. The shuttle took off straight up like a rocket, carrying a load of up to 24 tonnes. To land it swooped down to glide onto a runway.

# Living in space

**71** **Space is a dangerous place for astronauts.** It can be boiling hot in the sunshine or freezing cold in the Earth's shadow. There is also dangerous radiation from the Sun. Dust, rocks and bits from other rockets race through space at such speed, they could easily make a small hole in a spacecraft, letting the air leak out.

It is not easy for an astronaut wearing a bulky spacesuit to hold tools or bend his or her arms.

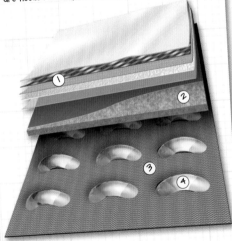

▼ In a spacesuit, many layers of different materials are needed to keep the astronaut safe.

## KEY
❶ Outer layers protect the wearer from the fierce heat of the Sun

❷ This layer seals the suit from the vacuum of space

❸ Soft lining goes next to the skin

❹ Tubes carrying cooling water

**72** **Spacesuits protect astronauts when they are out in space.** They are very bulky because they are made of many layers to make them strong. They must hold the air for astronauts to breathe and protect them against speeding dust and harmful radiation. To keep the astronauts cool while they work outside the spacecraft, tubes of water under the spacesuit carry away heat.

## SPACE MEALS

**You will need:**
dried noodles   boiling water
Buy a dried snack such as noodles, which just needs boiling water added. This is the kind of food astronauts eat. Most of their meals are dried so they are not too heavy to launch into space.

**73** Everything floats around in space as if it has no weight. So all objects have to be fixed down or they will float away. Astronauts have footholds to keep them still while they are working. They strap themselves into sleeping bags so they don't bump into things when they are asleep.

**74** Astronauts must take everything they need into space with them. Out in space there is no air, water or food, so all the things that astronauts need to live must be packed into their spacecraft and taken with them.

▶ Sleeping bags are fixed to walls so astronauts look as though they are asleep standing up.

# Home from home

**75** A space station is a home in space for astronauts and cosmonauts (Russian astronauts). It has a kitchen for making meals, and cabins with sleeping bags. There are toilets, wash basins and sometimes showers. There are places to work, and controls where astronauts can check that everything is working properly.

▼ The International Space Station provides astronauts with a home in space.

**76** Sixteen countries helped to build the International Space Station (ISS) in space. These include the US, Russia, Japan, Canada, Brazil and 11 European countries. It is built up from separate sections called modules that have been made to fit together like a jigsaw.

## I DON'T BELIEVE IT!

The US space station Skylab, launched in 1973, fell back to Earth in 1979. Most of it landed in the ocean but some pieces hit Australia.

KEY
1 Solar panels for power
2 Space shuttle
3 Docking port
4 Control module
5 Living module
6 Soyuz ferry

**77** Each part was launched from Earth and added to the ISS in space. There they were fitted by astronauts at the ISS with the help of a robot arm. Huge panels of solar cells have been added. These turn sunlight into electricity to provide a power supply for the space station.

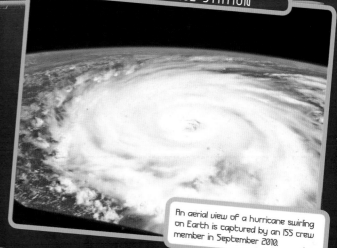

An aerial view of a hurricane swirling on Earth is captured by an ISS crew member in September 2010.

**78** The crew live on board the ISS for several months at a time. The first crew of three people arrived at the space station in November 2000 and stayed for over four months. The station now has sleeping quarters for six astronauts and many modules for living and working.

**79** People and supplies can travel to the ISS in Russian Soyuz spacecraft. There are also robot ferries with no crew, including Russian Progress craft and European ATVs (Automated Transfer Vehicles). In 2001, American Dennis Tito became the first space tourist, staying on the ISS for eight days.

# Robot explorers

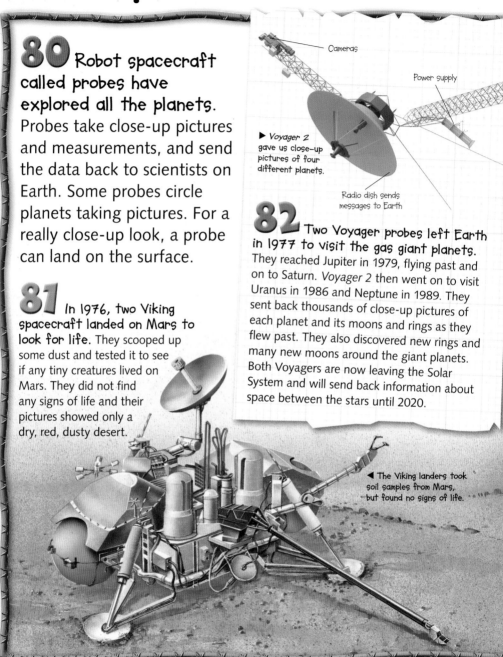

**80** Robot spacecraft called probes have explored all the planets. Probes take close-up pictures and measurements, and send the data back to scientists on Earth. Some probes circle planets taking pictures. For a really close-up look, a probe can land on the surface.

**81** In 1976, two Viking spacecraft landed on Mars to look for life. They scooped up some dust and tested it to see if any tiny creatures lived on Mars. They did not find any signs of life and their pictures showed only a dry, red, dusty desert.

Cameras

Power supply

▶ *Voyager 2* gave us close-up pictures of four different planets.

Radio dish sends messages to Earth

**82** Two Voyager probes left Earth in 1977 to visit the gas giant planets. They reached Jupiter in 1979, flying past and on to Saturn. *Voyager 2* then went on to visit Uranus in 1986 and Neptune in 1989. They sent back thousands of close-up pictures of each planet and its moons and rings as they flew past. They also discovered new rings and many new moons around the giant planets. Both Voyagers are now leaving the Solar System and will send back information about space between the stars until 2020.

◀ The Viking landers took soil samples from Mars, but found no signs of life.

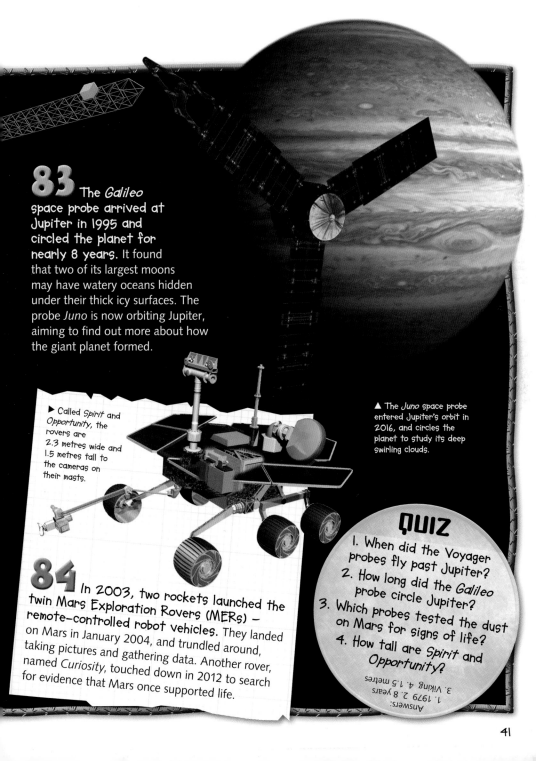

**83** The *Galileo* space probe arrived at Jupiter in 1995 and circled the planet for nearly 8 years. It found that two of its largest moons may have watery oceans hidden under their thick icy surfaces. The probe *Juno* is now orbiting Jupiter, aiming to find out more about how the giant planet formed.

► Called *Spirit* and *Opportunity*, the rovers are 2.3 metres wide and 1.5 metres tall to the cameras on their masts.

▲ The *Juno* space probe entered Jupiter's orbit in 2016, and circles the planet to study its deep swirling clouds.

**84** In 2003, two rockets launched the twin Mars Exploration Rovers (MERs) – remote-controlled robot vehicles. They landed on Mars in January 2004, and trundled around, taking pictures and gathering data. Another rover, named *Curiosity*, touched down in 2012 to search for evidence that Mars once supported life.

## QUIZ

1. When did the Voyager probes fly past Jupiter?
2. How long did the *Galileo* probe circle Jupiter?
3. Which probes tested the dust on Mars for signs of life?
4. How tall are *Spirit* and *Opportunity*?

Answers:
1. 1979 2. 8 years
3. Viking 4. 1.5 metres

# Watching the Earth

**85** Hundreds of satellites circle the Earth in space. They are launched into space by rockets and may stay there for ten years or more.

▼ Weather satellites look down at the clouds and give warning when a violent storm is approaching.

**86** Weather satellites help the forecasters tell us what the weather will be like. These satellites can see where the clouds are forming and which way they are going. They watch the winds and rain and measure how hot the air and the ground are.

▶ The different satellites each have their own job to do, looking at the Earth, or the weather, or out into space.

**87** Communications satellites carry TV programmes and telephone messages around the world. Large aerials on Earth beam radio signals up to a space satellite that then beams them down to another aerial, half way round the world. This lets us talk to people on the other side of the world, and watch events such as the Olympics Games while they are happening in faraway countries.

▼ Communications satellites can beam TV programmes directly to your home through your own aerial dish.

▶ Satellite telescopes let astronomers look far out into the Universe and discover what is out there.

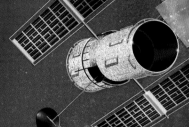

▼ Pictures of the Earth taken by satellites can help make very accurate maps.

**88** **Earth-watching satellites look out for pollution.** Oil slicks in the sea and dirty air over cities show up clearly in pictures from these satellites. They can help farmers by showing how well crops are growing and by looking for pests and diseases. Spotting forest fires and icebergs that may be a danger to ships is also easier from space.

**89** **Satellite telescopes let astronomers look at exciting things in space.** They can see other kinds of radiation, such as X-rays, as well as light. X-ray telescopes can tell astronomers where there may be a black hole.

# Voyage to the Moon

**90** **The first men landed on the Moon in 1969.**
They were two astronauts from the US *Apollo 11* mission.
Neil Armstrong was the first person
to set foot on the Moon. There
were five other Apollo mission that
landed on the Moon.

▲ In 1969, about half a billion people watched
U.S. astronaut Neil Armstrong's first steps
onto another world.

**91** **The giant *Saturn 5* rocket
launched the astronauts on their
journey to the Moon.** It was the largest
rocket to have ever been built. Its three
stages lifted the astronauts into space, and
the third stage gave it an extra boost to
send it to the Moon.

Thrusters

Command Module

Lunar Module

Legs folded
for journey

Main engine

Service Module
with fuel and air
supplies

▲ The Lunar and Command Modules
travelled to the Moon fixed together,
then separated for the Moon landing.

**92** **The Command Module that carried
the astronauts to the Moon had no more room
than an estate car.** The astronauts were squashed
inside it for the journey, which took three days to get
there and another three to get back. On their return,
the Command Module, with the astronauts inside,
splashed down in the sea.

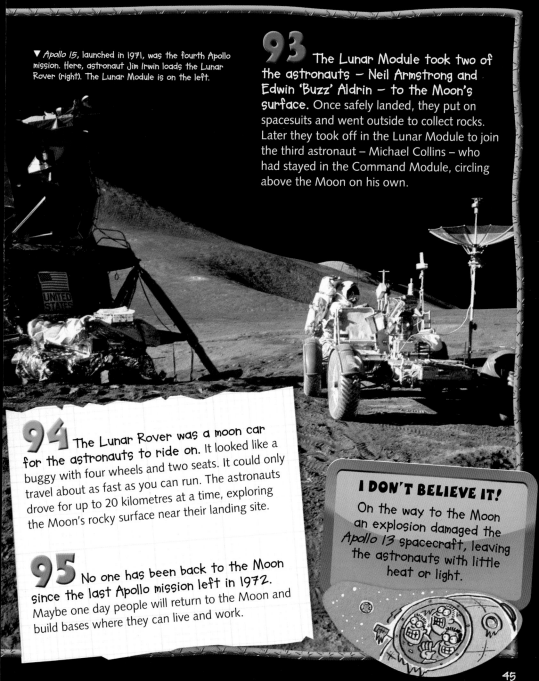

▼ *Apollo 15, launched in 1971, was the fourth Apollo mission. Here, astronaut Jim Irwin loads the Lunar Rover (right). The Lunar Module is on the left.*

**93** The Lunar Module took two of the astronauts – Neil Armstrong and Edwin 'Buzz' Aldrin – to the Moon's surface. Once safely landed, they put on spacesuits and went outside to collect rocks. Later they took off in the Lunar Module to join the third astronaut – Michael Collins – who had stayed in the Command Module, circling above the Moon on his own.

**94** The Lunar Rover was a moon car for the astronauts to ride on. It looked like a buggy with four wheels and two seats. It could only travel about as fast as you can run. The astronauts drove for up to 20 kilometres at a time, exploring the Moon's rocky surface near their landing site.

**95** No one has been back to the Moon since the last Apollo mission left in 1972. Maybe one day people will return to the Moon and build bases where they can live and work.

**I DON'T BELIEVE IT!**

On the way to the Moon an explosion damaged the Apollo 13 spacecraft, leaving the astronauts with little heat or light.

# Are we alone?

**96** The only life we have found so far in the Universe is here on Earth. Everywhere you look on Earth from the frozen Antarctic to the hottest, driest deserts, on land and in the sea, there are living things. Some are huge, such as whales and elephants, and others are much too small to see. But they all need water to live.

▼ On Earth, animals can live in a wide range of different habitats, such as in the sea, in deserts and jungles, and icy lands.

DESERT

SEA

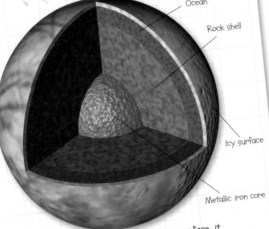

Ocean

Rock shell

Icy surface

Metallic iron core

▲ Deep beneath Europa's cracked, icy surface, it may be warm enough for the ice to melt into water.

POLAR LANDS

RAINFOREST

**97** There may be an underground ocean on Europa, one of Jupiter's moons. Europa is a little smaller than our Moon and is covered in ice. However, astronomers think that there may be an ocean of water under the ice. If so, there could be strange living creatures swimming around deep underground.

**98** Astronomers have found planets circling other stars, called exoplanets. Most of them are large, like Jupiter. But perhaps some could be smaller, like Earth. They could have a rocky surface that is not too hot or too cold, and suitable for liquid water – known as 'Goldilocks planets' after the fairytale character who tried the three bears' porridge. These planets could support some kind of life.

▲ No one knows what other exoplanets would be like. They could have strange moons or colourful rings. Anything that lives there might look very strange to us.

**99** Mars seems to have had rivers and seas billions of years ago. Astronomers can see dry riverbeds and ridges that look like ocean shores on its surface. This makes them think Mars may have been warm and wet long ago and something may once have lived there. Now it is very cold and dry with no sign of life.

**I DON'T BELIEVE IT!**
It would take thousands of years to get to the nearest stars with our present spacecraft.

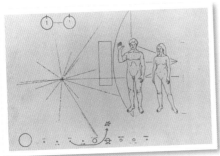

▲ Maybe the Pioneer plaques will be found by aliens who perhaps can read them and come to visit us!

**100** Each Pioneer probe carries a plaque about 23 centimetres wide. They show pictures of a man and woman, with the Solar System along the bottom and a chart of where the Earth is among the stars. In space the Pioneers will keep going forever, unless they hit something like a moon, a planet or an asteroid.

# Index

Page numbers in **bold** refer to main entries, those in *italics* refer to illustrations

## A

Aldrin, Edwin 'Buzz' 45
Apollo 11 44
Apollo 15 45
Apollo missions 44, 45, *45*
Armstrong, Neil 44, 45
asteroid belt 23
asteroids 11, **22–23**, *23*, 47
astronauts 6, *6*, 15, **36–37**, *36*, *37*, 38, *38*, 39, 44, *44*, 45, *45*
*Atlantis* 35
atmosphere *9*, 12
aurorae *20*

## B

Big Bang 30, *31*
black holes 27, *27*, 33, 43
booster rockets *34*, 35
Bullet Cluster *29*

## C

Cassiopeia A 27
Ceres 17, *17*
Chandra satellite 27
clouds 12, 14, 15, 18, *18*, 19, 20, 21, 24, 25, 28, 32, 33, 42, *42*
Collins, Michael 45
comets 11, **22–23**, *22*
Command Modules 44, *44*, 45
communications satellites 42, *42*
constellations 32, *32*
corona 9
cosmic microwave background 30
cosmonauts 38
craters 13, 16, *16*, 23
crust, Earth's *12*
Cygnus X-I 27

## D

dark matter 30
dust 11, 15, 22, 24, 30, 36, 40
dwarf planets 17, 21

## E

Earth 6, *6*, 8, 9, *9*, 10, *10*, 11, **12–13**, 14, 15, 16, 18, 23, 26, 30, 33, 34, 36, 39, *39*, 40, 42, *42–43*, *43*, 46, 47
elliptical galaxies 28, 29

Eris 17, *17*
Europa 46, *46*
exoplanets 47, *47*

## G

galaxies 6, **28–29**, *28*, *29*, 30, 31, 32
Galilean moons *18*
Galileo Galilei 18
*Galileo* space probe 41
gas 8, 9, 10, 11, 19, 20, 22, 24, 26, 27, *27*, 28, 30, 32, 33, 34, 40
gravity 10, 24, 27, 34
Great Red Spot 18, *18*

## H

Halley's comet 22
Haumea 17
Hubble Space Telescope 19, 33

## I

inner core, Earth's *12*
International Space Station (ISS) **38–39**, *38–39*
Io 18
irregular galaxies 29
Irwin, Jim 45

## J, K, L

*Juno* space probe 41, *41*
Jupiter *10–11*, **18–19**, *18*, 20, 23, *23*, 40, 41, *41*, 46, 47
Kuiper Belt 17
Lunar Modules 44, 45, *45*
Lunar Rover 45, *45*

## M

*Magellan* 14
Makemake 17
mantle, Earth's *12*
*Mariner 9* 15, *15*
Mars *10*, 11, **14–15**, *15*, 23, 40, *40*, 41, 47
Mars Exploration Rovers (MERs) 41
Mauna Kea observatory *32*
Mercury *10*, 11, 14, **16–17**, *16*, 26
meteors **22–23**
Milky Way Galaxy 26, 28, *28*, 29
Miranda *20*
Moon 9, *9*, 11, 13, *13*, 16, 17, **44–45**, *44*, *45*, 46
moons 11, 18, *18*, 19, 20, *20*, 40, 41, 46, 47, *47*

## N

nebulae 24, *24*, 25, 26, *26*
Neptune *11*, **20–21**, *21*, 22, 40
*New Horizons* 17

## O

Oberon 20
Olympus Mons 15
orbits 17, 20, 21, *21*, 38
*Orion* 32

## P

parachutes 35, *35*
Pioneer probes 47
planetary nebulae 26
planets 6, *6–7*, **10–11**, *10*, *11*, 12, *12*, *13*, 14, *14*, 15, *15*, 16, *16*, 17, 18, *18*, 19, *19*, 20, *20*, 21, *21*, 23, 24, 26, 30, 40, *40*, 41, *41*, 47
Pluto **16-17**, *17*, 21, *21*
pollution 43
probes 15, *15*, 17, 21, **40–41**, *41*, 47

## R

radio signals 33, 42
radio telescopes *33*
red giant stars 26, *26*
rings 19, *19*, 40, 47
robots 39, **40–41**
rockets **34–35**, *34*, 36, 41, 42, 44
Russia 38, 39

## S

satellite telescopes 43, *43*
satellites 27, 34, *34*, **42–43**, *42*, 43
Saturn 5 44
Saturn *11*, **18–19**, *19*, 20, 40
*Scorpius* 32
solar eclipses 9, *9*
solar flares 8, 9
solar panels *38–39*, 39
solar prominences 8, 9
Solar System **10–11**, 12, 17, 18, 20, 22, 47
solar wind 20
space shuttles 6, *34*, 35, *35*, 38
space stations 6, **38–39**, *38–39*
space tourists 39
spacesuits 6, 36, *36*, 45
spiral galaxies *29*
star clusters 25, *25*, 29

stars 6, 8, 17, 23, **24–25**, *24–25*, **26–27**, 28, *28*, 29, *29*, 30, 31, 32, 33, 40, 47
storms 15, *15*, 18, *18*, 21, 42
Sun **8–9**, *8*, 9, *10*, 11, 13, *13*, 14, 16, 17, 18, 20, 21, *21*, 23, 24, 25, 26, 28, 36
sunspots *8*, 9
supernovas 27, *27*

## T

telescopes 15, 19, 21, 27, **32–33**, *32*, *33*, 43, *43*
Titania 20
Tito, Dennis 39
TV 42

## U

Umbriel 20
Universe **30–31**, *30*, *31*, 43, 46
Uranus *11*, **20–21**, *20*, 40
USA 32, 35, 38, 39, 44

## V

Venus *10*, 11, **14–15**, *14*, 26
Viking spacecraft 40, *40*
volcanoes 12, *14*, 15, 18
*Voyager 2* 21, 40, *40*

## W

water 12, 14, 36, 41, 46, *46*, 47
weather 42
weather satellites 42, *42*
white dwarf stars 26, *26*
winds 15, 18, 42

## X

X-rays 27, 43
X-ray telescopes 43